Too Cool

Space Captain

Phil Kettle
illustrated by Craig Smith

Black Hills Publishing Pty Ltd
433 Wellington Street
Clifton Hill
Melbourne AUSTRALIA 3068

www.kidzbookhub.com.au
office@kidzbookhub.com.au

All rights reserved. No part of this publication may be reproduced
or transmitted in any form or by any means, electronic or
mechanical, including photocopying, recording, storage in an
information retrieval system, or otherwise, without the written
permission of the publisher, unless specifically permitted under
the Australian Copyright Act 1968 as amended.

ISBN: 9781920924171

A catalogue record for this
work is available from the
National Library of Australia

Contents

Chapter 1
Alien Threat — 1

Chapter 2
Countdown — 6

Chapter 3
Prepare to Launch — 11

Chapter 4
Invasion! — 14

Chapter 5
Alien Attack — 18

Chapter 6
Earth Is Saved — 24

Toocool's Alien Glossary	29
Toocool's Map	30
Toocool's Quick Summary	32
The Spaceship	34
Q & A with Toocool	36
Space Quiz	40

Chapter 1
Alien Threat

I was waiting for the signal. Earth was about to be invaded by cruel aliens. The world was depending on me, the greatest alien fighter that had ever lived.

The two-way radio beside my bed crackled before bursting into life. "Roberto to Toocool. Come in. Over."

I immediately picked up my two-way radio.

"Captain Toocool to Private Roberto. Over."

"Who made you captain?" said Roberto. "If you're captain, I'm not coming over, and then it *will* be over... and out. Over."

I thought for a moment.

"We can both be captains," I said, "but if there's an important decision to be made, then I'll make it. Over."

"Well, if there's an important decision to be made, we'll figure it out then. Over."

I knew if a decision had to be made, Captain Toocool would be the one to decide.

"Have you been contacted yet?" asked Roberto. "Over."

"Yes. Contact has been made. An attack from the aliens should begin in one hour. Over."

"I'll meet you at the spaceship in fifty minutes. Captain Roberto signing off. Over and out."

Chapter 2
Countdown

I changed into my space suit, which kind of looked like my track and field uniform. I grabbed my bike helmet and goggles.

Mom called out, "Toocool, your breakfast is on the table. Hurry up and make your bed."

I may be the captain of the greatest spaceship ever built, but Mom's the captain when I'm at home.

I looked out the window. No sign of the aliens yet, but they couldn't be far away.

During breakfast there was a knock on the back door. It was Marcy.

"What are you doing today, Toocool?"

"Roberto and I are astronauts today. We're flying into space to fight aliens from Planet Acne."

Marcy shut the door. I could hear her laughing as she walked away. Could Marcy be an Acne alien scout? I'd often thought that she came from another planet. There was no time to waste.

"Toocool, brush your teeth and comb your hair before you even think about going outside," said Mom.

She was right. I needed to look my best. Roberto and I would be heroes when we defeated the aliens. Our photo would be on the front page of every newspaper.

Chapter 3
Prepare to Launch

Roberto was already waiting outside the spaceship hangar. The spaceship was made from boxes we'd found in the shed. It had taken a whole day to build. Our spaceship was designed for speed. We couldn't risk being captured by those vicious aliens.

Even though we were both captains, I knew I was the only one who could make the big decisions.

"Are you ready to go, Captain?" I asked Roberto.

"Yes I am, Captain," he answered.

The launchpad looked like a seesaw, made from a plank of wood and a paint can from the toolshed.

"Time to move the spaceship onto the launchpad," I said.

We tied the spaceship onto my skateboard. Then we rolled it onto the launchpad. Private Bert the Rooster hopped in for a final flight check.

Chapter 4
Invasion!

Mr. Lopez looked at us from over the fence.

"What now?" he asked.

"We're just about to launch our spaceship," I said.

"I'd better get the first aid kit," said Mr. Lopez.

It was a good idea. The Acne aliens burst like pimples when they are hit. Their acid destroys anything it touches.

My two-way radio crackled.

"Captain, the word has just come through. The aliens are on the way. Over," said Roberto.

"Right, Captain. Over and out."

Roberto made sure our bucket of weapons was ready. Lemons are the perfect weapon to stop Acne aliens.

Private Bert the Rooster had finished the flight check. The rest of the crew joined him in the spaceship.

"Why do you get to sit in the front?" said Roberto.

"Because I got up here first," I said.

"Well, I'm going to sit in the front on the trip back," he replied.

"Start the engines," I said.

Before the engines started, something hit the spacecraft. It exploded and splashed juice all over us. It looked and tasted a lot like orange juice.

"We're too late," said Roberto. "The aliens are attacking."

Chapter 5
Alien Attack

It looked as if they'd landed in Marcy's backyard.

I looked over to Marcy's favorite climbing tree. Sure enough, the Acne aliens had made the tree their base, and they looked a lot like Marcy and Scott. They were armed with orange bombs.

"Attack! Attack!" I yelled.

Roberto fired the first lemon. It landed close to Alien Marcy.

"Take that, Acne aliens," I yelled, as I instantly threw another lemon.

It knocked the hat off the alien that looked like Scott. Their orange assault came back at us, thick and fast.

Alien Marcy yelled, "When you get out of that spaceship, I'm going to squash you like a lemon!"

Officer Dog was barking orders.

The next lemon grenade was rotten. It sailed though the air and made a direct hit, right on top of Alien Marcy's head.

Roberto and I both stood up and started to cheer. Dog barked happily. Our spaceship was really rocking now.

"I don't think I can hold the spaceship together much longer, Captain," I yelled.

"We're going to be killed," yelled Roberto.

"Never fear," I yelled. I knew at that moment that I was the real captain. I wasn't scared at all. "Abandon ship."

Roberto, Dog, and I jumped from the spaceship, landing on the other end of the wooden plank. This made our spaceship eject off the launchpad into the air.

It looked like Private Bert the Rooster, still inside the ship, was attempting an emergency landing.

Chapter 6
Earth Is Saved

Roberto and I rushed to the fence and looked over into Mr. Lopez's garden. The spaceship had landed on his tomato plants.

Our bomb-proof spaceship was not landing-proof. It had shattered on impact. Bert the Rooster was checking the damage to the landing site.

"Are you okay, Captain?" I asked Roberto.

"Yes. Are you okay, Captain?" he asked me.

I gave a thumbs-up sign.

Mr. Lopez took off his gardening gloves and threw them onto the ground.

"No, no, no," he said.

I could hear laughter from Marcy's backyard.

Then the captain of the house ordered Roberto and me inside for a full report.

The most important thing was that Roberto and I had saved Earth from the Acne aliens.

With Captain Toocool on board, the aliens never had a chance. I had put their vile plans on ice... for good.

The End!

Toocool's
Alien Glossary

Aliens—Creatures from outer space.

Assault—A military attack against enemy forces.

Astronaut—Someone who has been trained to travel into space.

Invasion—An enemy attack to take over a place, usually with force.

Launchpad—A base from which a rocket or spaceship is launched.

Vile—Rotten, horrible, and just plain wrong.

Toocool's Map
The Solar System

Toocool's Quick Summary
Trainee Astronauts

Did you know that people used to think that Earth was the center of the universe? For thousands of years, people thought the Sun revolved around Earth. Then, in the 1500s, a guy named Copernicus said that Earth moved around the Sun. It was a while before everyone believed him, though.

The word "astronaut" comes from two Greek words meaning "star sailor." When I learned that, I just knew that I would be an awesome astronaut.

To be an astronaut you must be good at math and science, and you should read everything that you can about astronauts and space in general.

You also need to be a team player like I am. I work really well on my own, but I also know how to tell other people what to do.

NASA chooses about a hundred people every few years to be part of an astronaut-training program. There's probably a letter from NASA in my mailbox right now.

The **Spaceship**

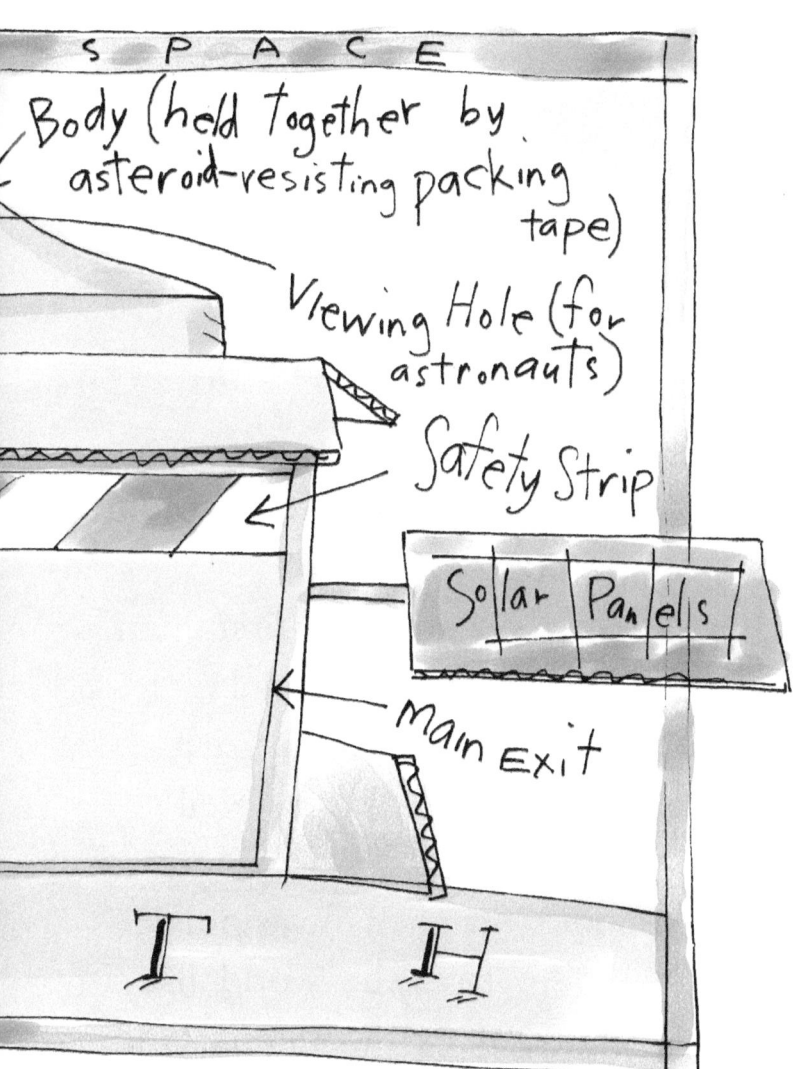

Q & A with Toocool
He Answers His Own Questions

Who is the greatest astronaut in the world?

Neil Armstrong was the first man to walk on the moon, and he wasn't bad, but he had a great crew. I only had Roberto. Neil Armstrong also didn't have to worry about an alien invasion. He wasn't out to save the world like I was. That takes extra courage and tactical genius.

What makes a good astronaut?

You need to be good at math and science, and you have to be really healthy. To be an astronaut, you also have to be in great shape. I have no trouble in that area after being number one in the world at nearly every sport I've ever tried.

Who first orbited Earth?

The *Sputnik 2* launched into space from Russia in 1957. It orbited Earth with its passenger, a dog named Laika. In Russia, astronauts are called cosmonauts, but I'm not sure what Laika would be called. Maybe a dogmonaut? It's a shame Dog wasn't alive then because he would have been famous.

Could you describe an astronaut's space suit?

NASA's space suits have twelve layers, and it takes astronauts forty-five minutes to put them on. Most of the layers are there for protection against extreme heat and cold. It can get pretty cold at TC Park in the winter, but not as cold as in outer space. The outside layer is made out of a mixture of fabrics. One of them is called Kevlar. Kevlar is so strong it is also used to make bullet-proof vests! The NASA space suits are really hard to get into. With the threat of an alien attack, I had to make do with my track uniform and goggles.

What is it like floating around in zero gravity?
Floating in space is fun. It's sort of like swimming underwater, only you don't get wet. Experienced astronauts like me don't call it zero gravity. I call it microgravity, or micro-g for short.

If there were another alien attack, would you volunteer your services to NASA?
Definitely. They would need someone with my experience. I've defeated aliens once, and I know I could do it again. It would probably also help the other astronauts to have someone on their team as fearless and skillful as I am.

Space Quiz
How Much Do You Know about Space Travel?

Q1 What do you need to do to be a great astronaut?
A. Look great with a fishbowl on your head. *B.* Work hard at math and science in school.
C. Watch a lot of science fiction on TV.

Q2 What is a Russian space traveler called?
A. Cosmonaut. *B.* Astronaut.
C. Space Legend.

Q3 How many planets are there in our solar system?
A. 9. ***B.*** 22. ***C.*** 50.

Q4 Which planet is closest to Earth?
A. Venus. ***B.*** Pluto. ***C.*** Acne.

Q5 What do you need to travel into outer space?
A. A space shuttle. ***B.*** A helicopter. ***C.*** You need to wish on a star.

Q6 What does *NASA* stand for?
A. Not Another Scary Alien.
B. National Aeronautics and Space Administration. ***C.*** National Academy of Super Aliens.

Q7 What is Earth's moon made of?
A. Cheese. **B.** Rock and dust.
C. A balloon.

Q8 What is the largest object in the solar system?
A. The Sun. **B.** Pluto.
C. Mr. Lopez's tomato plant.

Q9 What is the Sun?
A. A galaxy. **B.** A star. **C.** A moon.

Q10 Who will be the first person to walk on Mars?
A. Mr. Lopez. **B.** Toocool.
C. Marcy.

ANSWERS

- **1** B.
- **2** A.
- **3** A.
- **4** A.
- **5** A.
- **6** B.
- **7** B.
- **8** A.
- **9** B.
- **10** B.

If you got ten questions right, your letter from NASA will be in the mail. If you got more than five right, practice your moon walk. If you got fewer than five right, keep your feet on the ground and leave it to the experts.

Daredevil on Ice

Toocool and the Park Legends have trained hard, but the Westside Winners won't give up the hockey game without a fight. Has **Toocool** met his match?

Titles in the Toocool series

Slam Dunk Magician *Gocart Genius*
Fishing Fanatic *Invincible Iron Man*
BMX Champ *Soccer Superstar*
Surfing Pro *Baseball's Best*
Tennis Ace *Water Slide Winner*
Skateboard Standout *Beach Patrol*
Golfing Giant *Rodeo Cowboy*
Football Legend *Space Captain*
Sonic Mountain Bike *Daredevil on Ice*
Supreme Sailor *Discus Dynamo*

www.ingramcontent.com/pod-product-compliance
Lightning Source LLC
Chambersburg PA
CBHW021125080526
44587CB00010B/641